Firefighters

by Christopher Mitten

SCHOLASTIC INC.
New York Toronto London Auckland Sydney
Mexico City New Delhi Hong Kong Buenos Aires

Developed by Kirchoff/Wohlberg, Inc., in cooperation with Scholastic Inc.
Credits appear on the inside back cover, which constitutes an extension of this copyright page.

ISBN 0-439-35096-4

24 25 40 17 16 15 14

Who helps when there is a fire? Who puts the fire out?

Firefighters do!

First, firefighters try to save people from fires. They save homes from fires. They keep fires from spreading from house to house. They teach people about fire safety.

Buckets

Long ago, neighbors usually helped put out fires. They got water from a well. They used buckets for the water. They made two lines from the well to the fire. One line passed buckets full of water. The last person put water on the fire. The other line passed empty buckets back.

Fire Departments

After 1850, many cities had fire departments. The fire departments had new equipment. They didn't use just buckets.

They had water wagons to take water close to the fire. Horses pulled the wagons. There were rubber hoses on the wagons. Firefighters used the hoses to put water on the fire.

Firefighters Today

Fire fighting has changed. There are no more water wagons and horses.

Today firefighters have modern equipment. They get to a fire fast. They know the best ways to put out a fire.

The Fire Truck

The most important kind of equipment is the fire truck. Fire trucks take firefighters to a fire. Some fire trucks carry huge ladders. Other trucks carry long hoses. The trucks carry safety equipment too.

Other Equipment

People who fight fires have coats to keep fire away from them. They have hats that protect them too. They have masks to keep smoke away.

Firefighters have axes for breaking down doors. They use radios to talk to each other.

At the Firehouse

Firefighters stay at the fire station. They eat there. They sleep there. They check their gear. They fix their gear. They check the things they wear. They keep things they need ready.

They wait for a call. A call tells them there is a fire. Until then firefighters relax.

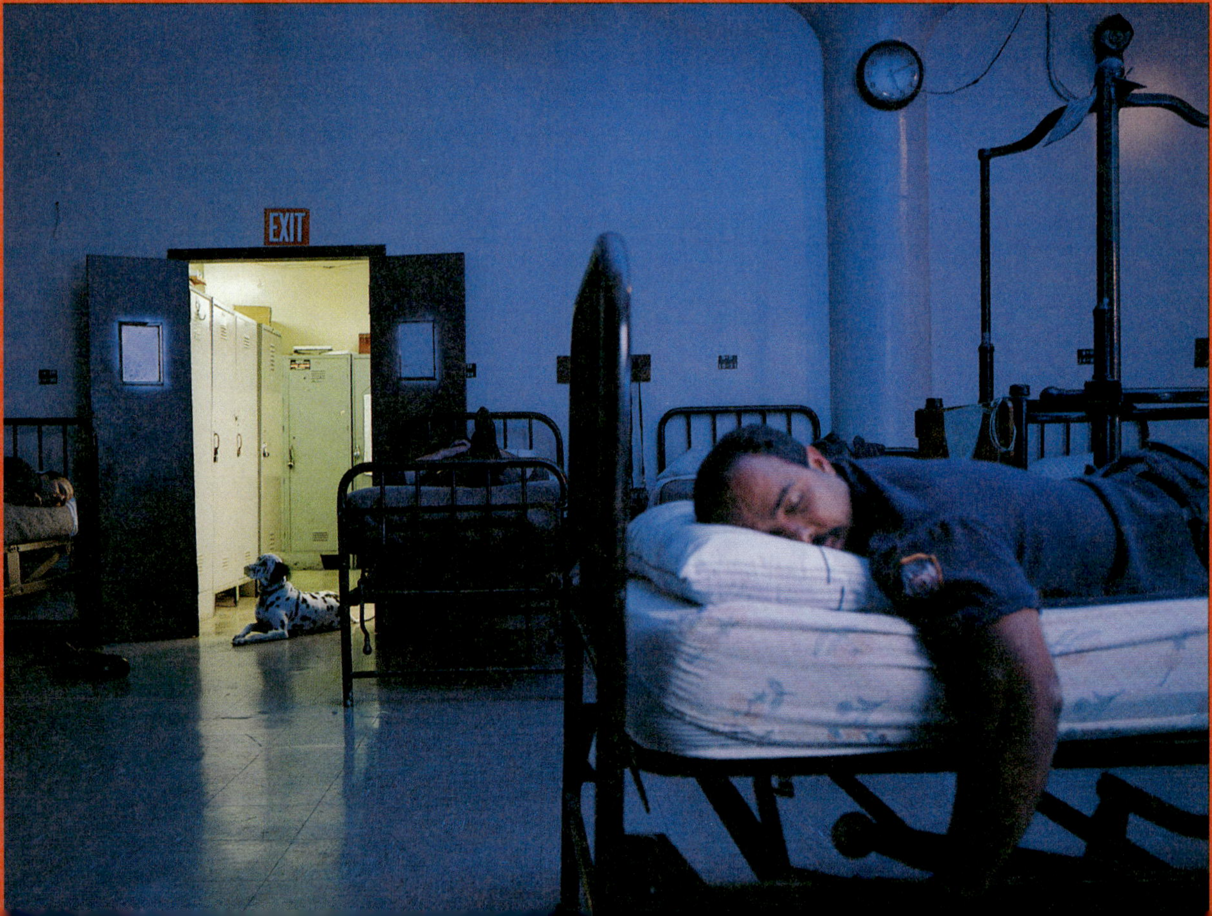

The Call!

When a call comes in, everyone moves fast. They get on the fire trucks. They put on their coats and hats.

Every minute counts! Drivers know the fastest way to get to the fire. Fire trucks have sirens. The sirens tell other drivers to let the fire trucks pass. Cars and trucks pull over to one side.

Fire!

At a fire, the fire chief tells firefighters what to do. The first thing to do is to save the people. Firefighters look for people who need help. They climb up ladders to save them. They may chop down doors to save the people.

The Last Flame

Other firefighters find the water hydrant. They connect the hose to it. They use hoses and pumps to put water on the flames. Water puts out fire.

After a fire, firefighters check everywhere. They make sure that every flame is out.

Forest Fires

Sometimes forests catch fire. Forest fires burn down trees. A forest fire can kill many animals and birds.

Special firefighters fight forest fires. These men and women have special training. They learn how to get water to a forest fire.

Sometimes trucks carry water to the fire. Sometimes helicopters are used. They carry water and drop it on the fire.

Fire on the Water!

Fires can happen on rivers or lakes. Boats can catch fire. Docks can catch fire too. When that happens, fireboats are called to fight the fire.

Fireboats are like floating fire trucks. They go to burning boats. They put out fires with water from the river or lake.

Off to School

Firefighters go to firefighting school. At school, they learn how to help people. They learn how to use their gear. They learn how to put out flames. They learn about fire safety.

Fire Safety

Firefighters teach people about fire safety. They go to schools and offices. They wear uniforms. Their uniforms are usually blue.

In schools, firefighters teach children about fire. They tell what to do in case of fire. They also teach ways to keep fires from starting.

Safety Tips

Here are some things to help keep you safe.

* Know how to call for help.
* Have smoke detectors. Make sure they work.
* Learn a safe way to get out in case of fire.